Reason and the World:
A Critical Thinking Workbook

Second Edition

Peter Vernezze
Weber State Unversity

KENDALL/HUNT PUBLISHING COMPANY
4050 Westmark Drive   Dubuque, Iowa 52002

Contents

Preface

This book arises out of a dissatisfaction--a dissatisfaction with the inability of most practical reasoning texts to address themselves to the discussion of contemporary issues that confront rational citizens. This shortcoming, which will come as no surprise to those familiar with such books, happens for the following reason. The notion of "practical" reasoning is usually opposed to that of "formal" reasoning. Since the latter textbooks are concerned with the abstract analysis of structure, it is thought sufficient if practical reasoning books examine actual written arguments. As a result, it seems that authors decide that any argument will do: arguments from psychology textbooks, from historical treatises, and all too often from actual philosophy articles (yuck!). The connection of such material to contemporary social and political debates is at best remote.

The worst illustration of how far critical thinking books are removed from reality comes in the treatment of fallacies. Ranging from the mundane to the absurd, the fallacy examples are either so ludicrous that the student doubts whether such things exist or so obvious that the student wonders why one troubles with them. But since fallacies not only abound but are far more subtle and successful than these books make them out to be (witness any political campaign), the student comes away with a decidedly misinformed view of the world.

Reason and the World attempts to remedy this deficiency by concerning itself with the application of reason to the world as we experience it. The general strategy of this book is to enable students to apply the skills they develop to issues of current political and social discourse. In this book students encounter

> **EXAMPLES drawn from the "real life" texts-- newspaper and magazine editorials, news programs, legal cases and political debates

> **EXERCISES involving the application of reasoning tools to current political and social issues

> **ARGUMENT ANALYSIS that demonstrates how a basic grasp of the argumentative process not only enriches one's understanding of current affairs but also allows one to interpret such events with a critical eye

The goal is to impart skills students can use to analyze the world of argumentation that actually does confront them, rather than the one that many practical reasoning books would have them believe confronts them. If reason is to be "practical" it must not concern itself only with words rather than with form, but with contemporary issues that face our society.

In **Chapter 1** some preliminary yet necessary delineations are drawn: the distinction between explanation and argumentation, and the distinction between premises and conclusions. In addition, the rudiments of argumentative form are developed. Exercises attempt to focus the student on what the point of an argument is and on how the components go together to advance that point.

Chapter 2 builds on the basics of argumentative form presented in the first chapter. This chapter demonstrates how the concept of argumentative form applies to arguments in everyday social and political discourse.

Chapters 3, 4, and 5 offer a three-step method of argument analysis. Students are asked to determine (a) whether any fallacies are committed, (b) whether the form of the argument is valid, and (c) whether the premises are true. It is the last of these, of course, that presents the greatest challenge. Both fallacies and form are relatively easy to point out, but the truth of the premises is a source of dispute. The method of argument analysis not only enables the student to recognize controversial premises, but it also provides a way by which one can either defend or criticize such premises.

Chapter 6 draws these separate pieces together and demonstrates the analysis of extended arguments. The examples vary from short, straightforward arguments to more elaborate editorials that require a more thorough and protracted analysis. In the spirit of the book, all of the examples are drawn from discussion of relevant social issues, and an attempt is made to present a balanced picture.

It is hoped that students will continue to develop the critical thinking skills throughout their college and professional careers. For critical thinking is not an activity one ceases at the end of a course of study, but an approach the student must carry out into the world if society is to progress. The world in general and a democratic society in particular need critical thought applied to all sides of any issue.

Reason and the World is a product of teaching critical thinking to undergraduates over a period of eight years at the University of Illinois at Chicago, the University of Washington, University of Maine at Farmington and Weber State University in Ogden, Utah. It owes its development and shape to the students in those courses. I would like to give a special thanks to Weber State University for presenting me with a Hemingway Faculty Development Award that allowed me the time required to finish the book and implement it into in my own critical thinking course. Finally, I would like to thank Madeleine Vernezze for her invaluable work in the editing of this book for publication and Elizabeth Ryan-Jeppsen for her tireless effort in the preparation of this manuscript.

Peter Vernezze

1

PRELIMINARIES

The Study of Critical Thinking

To study critical thinking as a separate discipline may strike you as a strange endeavor. If you enroll in a course on botany, biology, or physics, for example, it is assumed that you are taking the course in order to learn something you don't already know. But to apply the same rationale to a critical thinking course suggests a seemingly ludicrous conclusion; for it implies that you are taking the course in order to learn how to think! Clearly, you didn't get this far in your life without learning how to think. So the question remains: *What is the reason for taking a critical thinking course?*

I think that an easy answer can be given here, but it requires that we find another example. Rather than utilizing the comparison of a student entering an unfamiliar subject, a better analogy is that of an aspiring musician. Although she has some innate musical ability and already knows how to manipulate the instrument, she is far from reaching the level of ability of which she is capable. This will require hard work, dedication and time. In the same way, we all possess a modicum of reasoning skills. But

1

it is also clear that like the musician we are far from reaching the level of reasoning ability of which we are capable. In order to attain this goal we will likewise require hard work, dedication and time. Hence, we can say that although we all know how to think, a course in critical thinking can allow us to develop and refine those skills you already have. This modest proposition is the goal of this course.

Reasoning skills do not exist in a vacuum. Like any ability, we are going to want to develop them toward some purpose. We desire math skills so that we will be able to balance our checkbooks, to calculate interest rates, to compare mortgages. We acquire foreign language skills to be able to converse in a foreign country, to book a hotel room, to order dinner in a restaurant. *Why should we want to improve our reasoning skills?*

I have my own answer to this question, and it determines the design of this book. Simply stated this country needs our reasoning skills if it is going to survive as a democracy. What is a democracy? A democracy is a political organization in which we, the people, decide what is going to be the case. Not only by our votes at the polling booths but also by our views expressed in public forums, petitions, and letters, we decide whether we go to war, legalize abortions, institute affirmative action, provide aid to other countries.

How do we decide these things? Well, we can look at how they are being decided at present. Rather than engage in serious public dialogue on important issues, political campaigns are composed of sound bites and slick political advertisements. The two presidential candidates do not debate each other; rather, they hold, as one commentator correctly dubbed them, "joint press conferences," answering questions from prepared scripts, never daring to engage each other in a substantive exchange of ideas or a defense of principles. That would be too risky and might require some thought.

2

And it's not just political candidates who are guilty of this mindlessness and irrationality with regard to crucial issues. We ourselves engage in it. Rather than discuss the justifications for and against war, we either wave the flag or hoist protest banners; rather than debate the moral and social implications of abortions, we blow up clinics and physically block their use. All of these are acts that can be performed by your less than average chimpanzee; none of these are acts that utilize our mind.

The point of departure for this book is the conviction that what our democracy needs is an informed and rational exchange on the issues that confront us. It is the goal of this book to develop the reasoning skills that not only will produce better students, but better citizens as well. If a democracy is to survive, it requires a rational exchange of views, a nondogmatic and informed discussion of issues. A knowledge of the argumentative process and an ability to recognize, analyze, evaluate and write arguments is a necessary prerequisite to engaging in this exchange. In improving our logical skills we improve ourselves.

※   ※   ※

EXERCISE 1.1

If we wish to engage in an intelligent, rational debate on the issues that confront us, we will not only need to be informed about world events, but we must also be familiar with the method of logic which is at the heart of rational discourse. Full participation in the political dialogue requires we be able to combine these two skills.

PART I: THE FORM In each of the following, determine which statement (if any) follows logically from the first couple of statements given. Assume for the sake of the argument that the original statements are true.

1. All members of the President's Cabinet are lawyers.
    Some lawyers are male. Therefore,

    a. Some members of the President's cabinet are male

    b. Some members of the President's cabinet are not
       male

    c. All members of the President's cabinet are male

    d. None of the above

2. Ralph: All Italians enjoy spaghetti
   James: I have to disagree. I have known some Italians
   who loved baked potatoes.

   James's response shows that he has interpreted Ralph's
       remarks to mean that:

    a. Italians do not like potatoes

    b. Only Italians eat potatoes

    c. Most people cannot appreciate good spaghetti

    d. Only Italians enjoy spaghetti

    e. Italians enjoy only spaghetti

                          [From LSAT preparation book]

3. Anyone caught exposing himself to others in a theater
   can be arrested for indecent exposure. Pee Wee was
   not caught exposing himself to others in a theater.
   Therefore,

    a. Pee Wee can be arrested for indecent exposure

    b. Pee Wee can't be arrested for indecent exposure

    c. Pee Wee is innocent

    d. None of the above

4. If the makeup of the Supreme Court shifts, then Roe v. Wade will be overturned. The makeup of the Supreme Court did not shift. Therefore,

    a. Roe v. Wade will be overturned

    b. Roe v. Wade will not be overturned

    c. Roe v. Wade will be affirmed

    d. None of the above

5. Only language users employ generalizations. Not a single animal uses language. At least some animals reason. Therefore,

    a. Not all reasoning beings employ generalizations

    b. Only reasoning beings employ generalizations

    c. No reasoning beings employ generalizations

    d. None of the above

Part II: THE FACTS Briefly answer the following.

1. Name (a) your United States' Senators (b) the chief justice of the Supreme Court (c) one member of the president's cabinet.

2. What is the current law of the land on abortion? on capital punishment?

5

3. Discuss in brief one Supreme Court ruling from the recent term.

4. What freedoms are guaranteed by the First Amendment to the Constitution?

5. Briefly describe a current news story from each of the following regions:

   a. the Middle-East

   b. Africa

   c. Asia/South Pacific

   d. Latin America/South America

<u>Part III: PUTTING IT TOGETHER</u> On a separate sheet of paper, write a paragraph defending your views on one of the following topics.

a.   Should flag burning be constitutionally protected?

b.   Ought women be allowed in combat?

c.   Should a community have the right to outlaw nude dancing?

d.   Ought the police be able to stop you car at random in order to check your sobriety?

e.   Ought drugs be legalized?

f.   Should the terms of elected representatives be limited by law?

Argumentation and Explanation

Since this course will be dealing primarily with arguments, we will begin by defining what an argument is and then <u>distinguish arguments</u> from other uses of language. Finally, we will identify the various parts of an argument. The rationale for this procedure is as follows: Just as in any study we need to be able to identify and define what a thing is before we can undertake the study of it (imagine, for example, trying to study botany without beginning by identifying and defining plants), so in the study of arguments we want to begin by being able to identify and define our subject matter.

An <u>argument</u> is a set of statements in which one or more of the statements is offered as <u>evidence</u> for another of the statements. The statements offered as evidence are called the premises. The statement which the premise(s) is trying to establish is called the conclusion. The primary purpose of an argument is to persuade. In an <u>explanation</u>, one or more statements is intended to <u>clarify</u> another statement. We will call the statement being

7

clarified the explanandum and the statements that are doing the clarifying as the explanator(s). The primary purpose of an explanation is to inform.

Consider the following statements, all from the same story:

(1)   [a] Critics in Congress are pushing the other way, trying to reverse Bush's policy in order to punish Bejing for its brutal treatment of pro-democracy students and its continued repression in Tibet. [b] Senate Majority leader George Mitchell introduced a bill that would end MFN [most favored nation status] in six months unless Bejing shows more respect for human rights.

(2)   [a] The Communists took power in Bejing in 1949, and then, contrary to General Douglas MacArthur's confident prediction, the Chinese People's Liberation Army entered the Korean War against U.N. forces in 1950. [b] Unremitting enmity continued until President Richard Nixon's triumphant visit to Bejing in 1972.

(3)   [a] Like Nixon, Bush calls China a force for "stability" in Asia. [b] In fact, China is visibly unstable. [c] The country has experienced "primarily chaos and confusion" in this century, says Richard Holbroke, former Assistant Secretary of State for East Asian and Pacific Affairs. (*Time*. 10 June 1991)

When we analyze these three paragraphs, we see that they illustrate distinct uses of the language. We can say that paragraph (2) is meant merely to describe events in China, in particular, to detail the historical march of events in that country. What you want to note in particular is that the two statements [a] and [b] stand in no special relationship to each other. In paragraph (1) the situation is somewhat different. Sentence [b] is clearly meant to clarify sentence [a]. That is, by declaring that

Sen. Mitchell has introduced a bill to end Most Favored Nation status, [b] is explaining in what way Congress is trying to reverse Bush's policy. We will call statement [a] the _explanandum_ (the thing to be explained) and statement [b] the _explanator_ (the thing doing the explaining).

Finally, paragraph (3) is attempting to do something radically different than either (1) or (2). In particular, sentence [c] is offering you a reason for accepting sentence [b]. That is, the author is trying to convince you that China is unstable by offering you the statement of an alleged expert in the field that it is engulfed in chaos. (We will talk later about whether this is in fact a good reason for accepting a statement). Paragraph (3) is giving you an argument. Notice, finally, the relationship between the sentences. Sentence [c] is offering you a reason for accepting sentence [b]. We will call sentence [c] the _premise_ and sentence [b] the _conclusion_.

The two primary uses we are focusing on in this chapter are explanation and argument, though we will briefly consider some other uses of language. In order to further delineate between these two uses of language, consider the following examples:

(1)   [a] Moscow's aid to Cuba is not what it used to be. [b] In decades past, the Soviet Union provided Cuba with 90% of its oil at rates well below the world price. [c] Moscow also bought Cuban sugar at three to five times the world levels and supplied military hardware free. [d] The total package used to be worth at least $5 billion a year. [e] Those days are gone with perestroika. [f] Moscow's deals with Havana are now on a hard-currency basis at prevailing world prices. [g] Under a 1991 agreement worth $3.8 billion, the Soviet Union is to deliver 70 million barrels of oil to Cuba and, in exchange, receive 4 million tons of sugar, plus citrus fruit, nickel and medical supplies. [h] Though the bookkeeping is in dollars, the deal is still mainly barter. (_Time_. 17 June 1991)

(2)   [a] The hopes that the Cuban leader is on the decline are based on [b] his isolation as the only Soviet ally outside Asia to resist market economies and increased personal liberties. [c] In addition, the Soviet Union may be less willing to bolster the struggling Cuban economy, making life more austere. (*New York Times*. 28 January 1991)

Paragraph (1) is an explanation. The explanandum is sentence [a], that Moscow's aid to Cuba is not what it used to be. Sentences [b]-[h]--the explanators--form a complex reasoning chain intended to explain exactly why Moscow's aid is not what it used to be. By contrast, paragraph (2) is attempting to offer reasons to establish the proposition that Castro is on the decline. Propositions [b] and [c] are the premises, declaring that the reason for [a]--that Castro is on the decline--is that he resists market economies, ignores personal liberties, and may have his aid from Moscow cut off. [b] and [c] are hence the premises for proposition [a], which is the conclusion.

One way to mark the differences between these two paragraphs is to notice that in paragraph (1) nothing is being argued for. It is an uncontroversial claim being backed by some rather straight forward facts. In paragraph (2), however, the author is attempting to establish a statement that no doubt many would find controversial, that Castro is on the decline. The attempt to establish a controversial statement is one of the characteristics of an argument. If you have any question about whether you are confronting an argument or an explanation, ask yourself whether anyone really would argue about the point at issue. If the answer is 'yes' you have an argument; if the answer is 'no' you probably have an explanation.

Premise and Conclusion Indicators

Often, arguments will contain key words that

will alert you to the fact that a premise or a conclusion is about to occur. Consider the sentence: "the tax increase should not go into effect because it hurts the middle class." In this sentence what follows the word "because" is the premise of an argument. That is, the claim "it hurts the middle class" is the reason being offered for accepting the claim that "the tax increase should not go into effect." We call "because" and words like it <u>premise indicators</u>. Or take the argument "Cutting the capital gains tax rate would stimulate the economy. Hence, we ought to do it." Here, what follows the word "hence" is the conclusion of the argument--we ought to do it (cut the capital gains tax rate). We call "hence" and words like that <u>conclusion indicators</u>. Here is a partial list of premise and conclusion indicators:

<u>Premise Indicators</u>

- since
- because
- for
- in that
- given that
- seeing that
- for the reason that
- may be inferred from

<u>Conclusion Indicators</u>

- therefore
- accordingly
- hence
- thus
- consequently
- we may infer
- it must be that
- implies that
- as a result
- we may conclude

Although these words will often occur in passages, many times arguments will contain neither premise nor conclusion indicators. Consider the following example: "The senator is a member of the National Rifle Association. He will vote against the gun ban." The passage contains an argument, but no premise or conclusion indicator is present. What one must do in cases like this is be able to see that the first sentence "the senator is a member of the National Rifle Association" is the reason being offered for the claim that the senator will vote against the gun ban. Hence, even though no indicator word is present we can see that the first sentence is the premise and the second sentence is the conclusion. So although indicator words are nice tools, we cannot always count on having them around.

❊   ❊   ❊

EXERCISE 1.2

In the following examples, state whether you have an explanation or an argument. If you have an explanation, state what you think is the explanandum; if you have an argument, state what you think is the conclusion.

1.   Today, I can report to you that the Soviet Union has taken a decision to reduce its armed forces. Within the next two years, their numerical strength will be reduced by 500,000 men. The numbers of conventional armaments will also be subsequently reduced. (Mikhail Gorbachev, 7 December 1989)

TYPE:

EXPLANANDUM/CONCLUSION:

2. Critics of NAFTA, the North American Free Trade Agreement, argue that since the average U.S. factory worker makes $16.17 an hour and the average Mexican factory worker makes $2.35, <u>hundreds of thousands of American jobs will flow down the drain</u> to Mexico. (*Washington Post*. 14 September 1993)

TYPE:

ARGUMENT

EXPLANANDUM/CONCLUSION:

3. The actual cuts won't take place for two years. And even if they do occur, the Russians will still be ahead in conventional forces. Hence, we should not offer troop cuts in response to Gorbachev's offer. (Rep. Les Aspen. *This Week with David Brinkley*. 15 December 1989)

TYPE:

ARGUMENT

EXPLANANDUM/CONCLUSION:

4.   Arab countries sharply criticized the U.S. downing
      of two Libyan jet fighters yesterday. PLO leader
      Yasser Arafat called the incident "very serious."
      Chedle Klibi, the Arab League's secretary general,
      demanded that the United states end acts of
      "provocation near the Libyan coasts." In Syria,
      state-run television called the incident "flagrant
      U.S. aggression." (*New York Times*. 11 April 1987)

      TYPE:

      Exp

      EXPLANANDUM/CONCLUSION:

5.   Litigation cannot explain the rise in medical
      costs. If it could, both the cost of litigation
      and the size of jury awards would have been
      increasing throughout the last few decades. But
      there is no evidence that this is so. (*New
      Republic*. 22 November 1993)

      TYPE:

      Argument

      EXPLANANDUM/CONCLUSION:

6. As negotiations proceeded last week, the deadly sport of Hide the Hostage began to resemble a sophisticated version of the children's game Operator. Each party to the negotiations, whether dealing openly or behind the scenes, relayed its demands to Javier Perez de Cuellar. The U.N. Secretary-General transmitted each message to a third party, who in turn cried, "Operator!" requesting that the communication be repeated, clarified or amplified. Perez de Cuellar then went back to the first party, bearing new details, fresh analysis and cajoling reassurances. (*Time*. 26 August 1991)

TYPE:

EXPLANANDUM/CONCLUSION:

7. Many people think of the Soviet Union as an economic midget because of the turmoil that has gripped its economy in recent years. But this perception is wrong. Although production is grossly inefficient and the standard of living has always been miserable, the Soviet Union was until recently the world's second largest economy. (*U.S. News and World Report*. 9 September 1991)

TYPE: *ARGUMENT*

EXPLANANDUM/CONCLUSION:

15

8. There are currently 40 million Americans in 2,347 urban and rural areas who do not have primary-care medicine. Nearly 11,000 primary care doctors are needed to help these communities reach the government's target rate of 1 doctor for every 2,000 residents. (*U. S. News and World Report*. 20 September 1993)

TYPE:

explan

EXPLANANDUM/CONCLUSION:

9. Despite evidence that Pakistan is developing nuclear weaponry, we should not cut off aid to Pakistan because it is strategically located and we have a relationship with them. We'd like Pakistan to stand by us in the Gulf crisis, for example. The fundamental point is to enforce the law to limit the spread of nuclear weapons, but the penalty in the law is extremely harsh. (*U.S. News and World Report*. 15 October 1990)

TYPE:

Argument

EXPLANANDUM/CONCLUSION:

10. The United States' Strategic Petroleum Reserve (SPR) is a government owned cache of nearly 600 million barrels tucked away in mammoth salt-dome caverns beneath the coastal plain of Texas and Louisiana. Established in 1975, the SPR's trove is intended to help the nation cope with any interruption in its energy supply. The oil held in the SPR represents a 2 1/2 month supply if the U.S. should lose the 8 million barrels of oil it imports each day. (*U.S. News and World Report*. 15 October 1991)

TYPE:

exp

EXPLANANDUM/CONCLUSION:

11. As a result of the Gulf crisis, a debate has broken out over whether or not to break into this stash. But as the energy experts and policy-makers see it tapping into the reserve makes good sense, since it would have a powerful psychological effect on jittery world markets--calming the nerves of oil traders and holding down inflationary fuel-price jumps. (*U.S. News and World Report*. 15 October 1991)

TYPE:

Argument

EXPLANANDUM/CONCLUSION:

12. The relative rate of growth of health care costs is indisputable. From 1948 to 1992 the price of a doctor's services increased more than 5.5 percent a year, compared with an average annual increase of 4 percent in the Consumer Price Index. (*New Republic*. 22 November 1993)

    TYPE:

    ARGUMENT

    EXPLANANDUM/CONCLUSION:

13. Some will argue that Star Wars, or the Strategic Defense Initiative (SDI), should not be undertaken because <u>it will breach or undermine the 1972 Anti-Ballistic Missile Treaty</u>, which prohibits the United States from deploying a territorial defense against long-range missiles. (*New Republic*. 8 February 1993)

    TYPE:

    ARGUMENT

    EXPLANANDUM/CONCLUSION:

14. But the Iraqis are notorious for making deals when cornered, then breaking them. In 1970, Baghdad granted Iraq's Kurdish minority the right to an autonomous region. Since then, Hussein has tried repeatedly to crush Kurdish nationalism. In 1975, Iraq signed an agreement with Iran to share the Chat al-Arab waterway that divides the two countries: five years later, Hussein invaded Iran. (*U.S. New and World Report*. 12 November 1990)

TYPE:

expl

EXPLANANDUM/CONCLUSION:

15. DeKlerk asked lawmakers to dismantle the Group Areas Act, which segregates black and white residential areas, and the Land Acts, which bar blacks from owning land outside specially designated homelands. He unveiled a major surprise by promising to phase out the infamous Population Registration Act. That hated law underpins the entire apartheid system by forcing South Africans to register by racial group for political and economic purposes. (*Time*. 11 January 1991)

TYPE:

OTHER

EXPLANANDUM/CONCLUSION:

16. The Swiss have also discovered they are not immune to the social ills that afflict others. The country has Europe's highest incidence of AIDS and a rising drug-related crime problem. In Zurich's Platzspitz, a sordid, officially sanctioned Needle Park nestles only a few minutes' walk from the banking district where the city's fabled gnomes control the levers of the national economy. (*Time*. 19 August 1991)

    TYPE:

    EXPLANANDUM/CONCLUSION:

17. Liberty finds no refuge in a jurisprudence of doubt. Yet 19 years after our holding that the Constitution protects a woman's right to terminate her pregnancy in its early stages, that definition of liberty is still questioned. Joining the respondents as amicus curiae, the United States, as it has done in five other cases in the last decade, again asks us to overrule Roe. (Supreme Court decision, *Planned Parenthood vs. Casey*)

    TYPE:

    EXPLANANDUM/CONCLUSION:

18. Of the Arab States, Jordan would appear to have the most to gain from peace with Israel. Lacking the oil wealth and military power of other Arab countries, it could benefit economically and strategically from cooperation with Israel. But the benefits would not outweigh the danger to King Hussein's regime. Jordan is already threatened by domestic fundamentalists, who won more seats than any other bloc in the newly reformed Jordanian parliament. Hence, Jordan will in all likelihood refuse the overtures of peace. (_New Republic_. 24 May 1993)

TYPE:

EXPLANANDUM/CONCLUSION:

19. Initiative A imposes, by law, term limits on United States Senators, United States Congressional Representatives, and on each elected state and county officer, except judges, unless the person running for that office held it on April 15, 1993. Initiative A also requires a run-off election for all races in which no candidate received a majority of the votes cast for that office. (from _Utah Ballot Initiative_)

TYPE:

EXPLANANDUM/CONCLUSION:

20. In Smith, the Court abandoned the test, except for the most blatant cases of religious discrimination. In a 5-4 decision, Justice Antonin Scalia held that there was no need to prove a compelling state interest "if prohibiting the exercise of religion...is not the object of a law but merely its incidental effect." (*New Republic*. 2 November 1992)

TYPE:

EXPLANANDUM/CONCLUSION:

21. Despite lapses into protectionism, the U.S. has generally been both a promoter and a beneficiary of free trade. It grants 159 of the 170 countries on earth most favored nation status, or MFN, subjecting their products to roughly the same relatively low import duties. (*Time*. 26 August 1991)

TYPE: *EXPLANATION*

EXPLANANDUM/CONCLUSION:

22. Totalitarian countries, however, are better at
    withstanding trade sanctions than democracies are
    at imposing them. Fidel Castro's regime, for one,
    has easily survived a 29 year ban on selling sugar,
    cigars or anything else to the U.S. (*Time*. 26
    August 1991)

    TYPE:

    EXPLANANDUM/CONCLUSION:

23. A major immigration commission was set up in 1978.
    Its recommendations were incorporated into the
    Immigration Reform Act of 1981. That act addressed
    the illegal immigration issue with a deal: those
    already here could apply to legalize their status,
    but further numbers of illegal immigrants would be
    stanched by imposing penalties on employers who
    hired illegal immigrants. (*New Republic*. 27
    December 1993)

    TYPE:

    EXPLANANDUM/CONCLUSION:

24. Why is the three strikes proposal a bad one? Only→ 1 percent of crimes are committed by people over 60; it makes sense to lock up violent offenders from ages 20 to 50, but not from 50 to 80; repeat offenders are already guaranteed long prison terms by U.S. sentencing guidelines, which require fifteen year sentences for someone who commits murder with two prior offenses. (*New Republic*. 21 March 1994)

    TYPE: *ARGUMENT*

    EXPLANANDUM/CONCLUSION:

    BAD PROPOSAL BECAUSE

25. The current Senate bill, however, includes a far more revolutionary amendment from Senator D'Amato. It would extend the federal death penalty to any murder committed with a gun that has "moved at any time in interstate or foreign commerce." (*New Republic*. 21 March 199/,

    TYPE:

    EXPLANANDUM/CONCLUSION:

EXERCISE 1.3

Pick up a newspaper or news magazine. Write down one story that provides an explanation and one story that gives argumentation.

Explanation:

Argumentation:

Turning reasons into arguments

In this book, we will be primarily concerned with argumentation. As stated previously, an argument contains two parts: a premise (or premises) and a conclusion. It is the relation between these two parts that will interest us here. Just as in a murder trial the prosecuting attorney might claim "the defendant was the last person seen leaving the murder scene, his fingerprints were on the weapon, and we know he had a deep hatred of the deceased" as reasons you should accept the conclusion that the defendant is guilty of murder, so in rational discourse someone might offer you the claim that "abortion is murder" as a reason for accepting the conclusion that abortion is wrong, or declare that "political speech is constitutionally protected" as a reason for accepting the conclusion that flag burning ought to be allowed. In these and in many other cases you will invariably confront, the first thing you want to see here is how such claims constitute arguments. Consider, for example, the following statement:

(1) We should go to war with Iraq because Hussein has violated the sovereignty of another nation.

In this passage you are being offered a reason (or premise) for accepting the conclusion that "we ought to go to war." An initial sketch of the reasoning would look like this.

    Premise: Hussein has violated the
                   <u>sovereignty of another nation</u>
    Conclusion: We should go to war with Iraq

Likewise, the following claim provides a reason that tries to persuade you of the opposite conclusion and should be analyzed as indicated.

(2) We should not go to war with Iraq since sanctions have not been allowed sufficient time to work.

  P: <u>Sanctions have not been allowed time to work</u>
  C: We should not go to war with Iraq

MODUS PONENS

Although these passages provide reasons for a conclusion, you do not yet have an argument; for the reasons or premises offered do not as yet logically guarantee the conclusion. In good arguments, the ones we are aiming to construct and the ones we hope to analyze, the premises offered guarantee the conclusion to the extent that if the premises are true then the conclusion is true. Indeed, the attribute of premises logically guaranteeing the conclusion is one that all good arguments must possess, for there is no reason for anyone to accept a claim unless the premises being offered logically guarantee the conclusion being argued for.

What this means, then, is that we must rewrite the passage in order to show the underlying logic of the argument, since as they stand they do not possess the logical structure we require. We will have to begin, then, by being overly elaborate and showing you all the parts of an argument in what may seem painstaking